Would You
Rather?
Christmas
EDITION

Would You Rather?

Christmas

EDITION

Laugh-Out-Loud
Holiday Game for Kids

LINDSEY DALY

Z KIDS · NEW YORK

Published in the United States by Z Kids, an imprint of Zeitgeist™, a division of Penguin Random House LLC, New York.

penguinrandomhouse.com

Zeitgeist™ is a trademark of Penguin Random House LLC

ISBN: 9780593435663
Ebook ISBN: 9780593435922

Cover art © by Budai Romi/Shutterstock.com,
In-Finity/Shutterstock.com, miumi/Shutterstock.com,
Nicoleta Ionescu/Shutterstock.com,
and mhatzapa/Shutterstock.com
Interior art © by mhatzapa/Shutterstock.com,
Freud/Shutterstock.com, and Tetyana P/Shutterstock.com
Author photograph by Jocelyn Morales
Book design by Erin Yeung

Printed in the United States of America

1 3 5 7 9 10 8 6 4 2

First Edition

For the Unity Charter School Class of 2022.
Being your teacher makes every day
feel like Christmas!

Ayana	Luis
Bowie	Lukas
Brielle	Max
Declan	Meggin
Hope	Minsi
Jack T.	Olin
Jack W.	Patrick
James	Raymond
Jayden	Rebecca
Lilah	Sam
Lizzie	Shohnaleigh
Lucia M.	Teddy
Lucia P.	

Contents

Introduction

There's a reason that the Christmas season is known as the best time of the year. It's filled with family, friends, food, and gifts. Throw in a break from school and what's not to love? Plus, there are so many fun activities at Christmas, like ice-skating, sledding, baking cookies, and, of course, a hilarious and thought-provoking game of "Would You Rather?"

You made priceless memories with your family and friends playing *Would You Rather? Made You Think! Edition* and *Family Challenge! Edition;* now you can have a blast during the holidays with over 160 all-new questions—but this time with a touch of Christmas magic!

Would You Rather? Christmas Edition is sure to spark unforgettable family conversations during the car ride to Grandma's house or when you're waiting for Christmas dinner. Each question is designed to make you think critically and start funny, thoughtful, and creative conversations. Not only do the questions inspire interesting dialogue and laughter, but they may also reveal fascinating details about how others think! Your competitors' responses may even change the way that you think about a certain topic.

This book can be played as a game, with players scoring each question. Nobody has an advantage over anyone else; any player, no matter their age, can win if they come up with the most imaginative and intriguing response. So put away the Christmas movies, because you have all the holiday entertainment you need right here!

Rules of the Game

Get a group of friends or family members together for a Christmas game of wits and creativity. The more the merrier!

* The game is played in 8 rounds with 20 questions in each round.

* Players rotate the responsibility of being the "judge" and read the question aloud to the group.

* Players will have one minute to develop their answer with an explanation.

* Players will take turns sharing their answers.

* The judge of that round will then select the answer that they enjoyed the most based on humor, creativity, or logic. The player whose answer was chosen will be awarded a point for that question.

* If only two people are playing, the judge (the player reading the question) assigns 1 to 5 points for the answer (5 being the best answer) and records it with the other player's name in the space provided below the question.

* When all players complete the round, tally up the points to determine the winner for that round.

* In the event of a tie at the end of a round, the two players who are tied will answer the tiebreaker question. All remaining players will vote on the best answer. If only two people are playing, whoever makes the other player laugh wins.

* When players complete the book, the winner of the most rounds is the champion!

ROUND

1

The Perfect Present

Would you rather
receive one large, expensive gift
or
ten small, cheap gifts?

WINNER: POINTS:

Would you rather
catch someone regifting
your present
or
returning it for something else
at the store?

WINNER: POINTS:

Would you rather
open a gift that is wrapped
in hot wax
or
duct tape?

WINNER: POINTS:

Would you rather
have to follow clues to
find your gift
or
create clues for someone
to find their gift from you?

WINNER: POINTS:

Would you rather
get a paper cut from
wrapping paper
or
get smacked in the face
with a gift box?

WINNER: POINTS:

Would you rather
receive a gift basket with
all your favorite food
or
a gift card to your
favorite restaurant?

GIFT
CARD

WINNER: POINTS:

Would you rather
be given five golden rings
or
a partridge in a pear tree?

WINNER: POINTS:

Would you rather
have to climb a mountain to
get your gift
or
dive into the depths of the ocean?

WINNER: POINTS:

Would you rather

receive 35 gifts that you can't open
until six months after Christmas

or

20 gifts that you can open right
away?

WINNER: POINTS:

Would you rather

wake up on Christmas
morning to a tower of gifts
as high as the ceiling

or

a new puppy?

WINNER: POINTS:

Would you rather
receive a tarantula
or
an ant farm?

WINNER: POINTS:

Would you rather
spend a day covered head to toe in
wrapping paper
or
trapped inside a large gift box?

WINNER: POINTS:

Would you rather
find a cockroach in
your stocking
or
a garden snake?

WINNER: POINTS:

Would you rather
never receive another
Christmas present again
or
receive only terrible presents?

WINNER: POINTS:

Would you rather
wrap 100 presents
or
stuff 100 gift bags?

WINNER: POINTS:

Would you rather
receive a great gift that you
have to share with a friend
or
an average gift that you can
keep for yourself?

WINNER: POINTS:

Would you rather
open your gifts a month before
Christmas on your own
or
around the tree on Christmas
morning with your family?

WINNER: POINTS:

Would you rather
receive a toy that takes hours
to put together
or
a video game that takes two days
to download?

WINNER: POINTS:

Would you rather
forget to buy a gift for someone
in your family
or
have them forget to buy you one?

WINNER: POINTS:

Would you rather
find coal in your stocking
or
a mouse eating all of your
stocking stuffers?

WINNER: POINTS:

Would you rather
be given $500 cash
or
a gift worth $750 that you
can't return or exchange?

WINNER: POINTS:

WINNER: _____

TOTAL POINTS: _____

ROUND

2

Deck the Halls

Would you rather
accidentally knock over a
friend's Christmas tree
or
tear down their light display?

WINNER: POINTS:

Would you rather
make your family
customized ornaments
or
stockings?

WINNER: POINTS:

Would you rather
sleep in a room surrounded
by evil nutcracker dolls
or
scary elves?

WINNER: POINTS:

Would you rather
chop down a Christmas tree
for your family
or
put Christmas lights on the roof?

WINNER: POINTS:

Would you rather
wear pants made of tinsel
or
mistletoe?

WINNER: POINTS:

Would you rather
get tangled in Christmas lights
or
fall into a pile of plastic ornaments?

WINNER: POINTS:

Would you rather
have the angel on top of the
Christmas tree come to life
or
the three wise men from
the nativity scene?

WINNER: POINTS:

Would you rather
decorate your lawn with
Christmas inflatables
or
create a light show set to music?

WINNER: POINTS:

Would you rather
jump into a pool filled
with poinsettias
or
boughs of holly?

WINNER: POINTS:

Would you rather
cover your living room in fake snow
or
real pine needles?

WINNER: POINTS:

Would you rather

own a massive collection of snow globes to display at Christmas

or

toy trains?

WINNER: POINTS:

Would you rather

keep your Christmas decorations up for an entire year

or

skip a year of decorating?

WINNER: POINTS:

Would you rather
get lost on a
Christmas tree farm
or
in a factory that makes
Christmas lights?

WINNER: POINTS:

Would you rather
wear a Christmas tree skirt
out in public
or
a shirt made of candy canes?

WINNER: POINTS:

Would you rather
get a mouthful of fake snow
or
real mistletoe?

WINNER: POINTS:

Would you rather
live in a life-size
gingerbread house
or
snow globe?

WINNER: POINTS:

Would you rather
construct a Christmas tree
out of paper towel rolls
or
popsicle sticks?

WINNER: POINTS:

 **Would you rather**
play a game of
ring toss using wreaths
or
horseshoes using
candy canes?

WINNER: POINTS:

Would you rather

use a creepy porcelain doll as your
Christmas tree topper

or

an embarrassing baby picture
of you?

WINNER: POINTS:

Would you rather

get a job designing miniature houses
for Christmas villages

or

toy train sets?

WINNER: POINTS:

Would you rather

pick up every pine needle that falls
off the Christmas tree by hand

or

polish each ornament with
a toothbrush?

WINNER: POINTS:

WINNER

ROUND

2

WINNER: _____

TOTAL POINTS: _____

ROUND

3

Eat, Drink, and Be Merry

Would you rather
drink spoiled eggnog
or
eat month-old fruitcake?

WINNER: POINTS:

Would you rather
eat a mashed potato–flavored
candy cane
or
a roast beef–flavored
Christmas cookie?

WINNER: POINTS:

Would you rather
eat an entire Christmas ham
by yourself
or
drink a gallon of gravy?

WINNER: POINTS:

Would you rather
take a bath in a tub of
hot roasted potatoes
or
sticky toffee pudding?

WINNER: POINTS:

Would you rather
eat a tuna fish–infused
gingerbread cookie
or
a snickerdoodle cookie topped
with ketchup?

WINNER: POINTS:

Would you rather
be allowed to eat only yams for
Christmas dinner
or
green bean casserole?

WINNER: POINTS:

Would you rather

have Christmas dinner with
Ebenezer Scrooge

or

bake Christmas cookies
with the Grinch?

WINNER: POINTS:

Would you rather

eat a carrot that's been slobbered
on by a reindeer

or

a Christmas cookie that Santa
sneezed on?

WINNER: POINTS:

Would you rather
drink hot apple cider
until you're sick
or
eggnog?

WINNER: POINTS:

Would you rather
eat figs
or
chocolate-covered
pine needles?

WINNER: POINTS:

Would you rather
eat turkey that's been burnt to a
crisp and steaming hot
or
undercooked and cold inside?

WINNER: POINTS:

Would you rather
be drenched in hot cocoa
or
iced peppermint coffee?

WINNER: POINTS:

Would you rather
wear body spray that
smells like gravy
or
roasted potatoes?

WINNER: POINTS:

Would you rather
eat a stale gingerbread house
or
expired figgy pudding?

WINNER: POINTS:

Would you rather
eat only peppermint bark for
an entire week
or
gumdrops?

WINNER: POINTS:

Would you rather
jump into a pile of cinnamon
or
stuffing?

WINNER: POINTS:

Would you rather
be hit in the face with
a warm apple pie
or
a cold cheesecake?

WINNER: POINTS:

Would you rather
dip your sugar cookies
in creamed spinach
or
cranberry sauce?

WINNER: POINTS:

WOULD YOU RATHER?

Would you rather
have Christmas dinner with someone
who chews with their mouth open
or
spits when they talk?

WINNER: POINTS:

Would you rather
cook Christmas dinner
for 20 people
or
bake pies for 100 people?

WINNER: POINTS:

Would you rather
participate in a pumpkin
pie-eating contest
or
a hot cocoa-drinking
competition?

WINNER: POINTS:

WINNER: _____

TOTAL POINTS: _____

ROUND

4

Ho Ho Holiday Traditions

Would you rather
meet Santa
or
take a ride on the Polar Express?

WINNER: POINTS:

Would you rather
wear an ugly Christmas sweater
every day for a year
or
elf ears?

WINNER: POINTS:

Would you rather
have your parents send a
Christmas card with a terrible
picture of you
or
embarrassing information
about you?

WINNER: POINTS:

Would you rather
have your room destroyed by
the Elf on the Shelf
or
discover that he drew on your face
with a permanent marker?

WINNER: POINTS:

Would you rather
pose for a photo in matching
Christmas pajamas with your family
or
dress up as Santa for your
family party?

WINNER: POINTS:

Would you rather
get front-row tickets to see
the Rockettes
or
the *Nutcracker* ballet?

WINNER: POINTS:

Would you rather
forget your favorite
Christmas memory
or
have it play endlessly in your
head on repeat?

WINNER: POINTS:

Would you rather
drive around looking at
Christmas lights
or
have a Christmas movie marathon?

WINNER: POINTS:

Would you rather

sit through a three-hour lecture on
the history of Christmas wreaths

or

advent calendars?

WINNER: POINTS:

Would you rather

play the piano for your family
on Christmas

or

have the starring role in a Christmas
play at church?

WINNER: POINTS:

Would you rather
go out in public dressed
as an angel
or
one of the three wise men?

WINNER: POINTS:

Would you rather
participate in a grab bag
gift exchange
or
a Secret Santa?

WINNER: POINTS:

Would you rather
help Santa deliver
gifts in his sleigh
or
spend a day in
his workshop?

WINNER: POINTS:

Would you rather
listen to a group of carolers
or
a gospel choir?

WINNER: POINTS:

Would you rather

play the role of the donkey in a Christmas pageant

or

baby Jesus?

WINNER: POINTS:

Would you rather

eat the traditional "Feast of the Seven Fishes" on Christmas Eve

or

a special breakfast on Christmas Day?

WINNER: POINTS:

Would you rather

discover that the treats in your advent calendar are chocolate-covered Brussels sprouts

or

garlic cloves?

WINNER: POINTS:

Would you rather

visit the Rockefeller Center Christmas tree in New York City

or

a Christmas market in Europe?

WINNER: POINTS:

Would you rather
make a Christmas-themed craft
or
bake snickerdoodle cookies
from scratch?

WINNER: POINTS:

Would you rather
wear fancy clothes for
Christmas dinner
or
pajamas?

WINNER: POINTS:

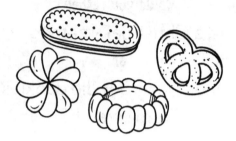

Would you rather
leave cookies and milk
for Santa
or
carrots for his reindeer?

WINNER: POINTS:

WINNER

ROUND 4

WINNER:
_____

TOTAL POINTS:
_____

ROUND

5

Christmas Classics

69

Would you rather

be visited by the ghosts of Christmas Past, Present, and Yet To Come from *A Christmas Carol*

or

spend a night in Whoville from *How the Grinch Stole Christmas*?

WINNER: POINTS:

Would you rather

go Christmas caroling with a group of people who sing out of tune

or

can't remember the lyrics to any of the songs?

WINNER: POINTS:

Would you rather
go ice-skating at
Rockefeller Center with
Buddy the Elf
or
Jack Skellington?

WINNER: POINTS:

Would you rather
listen to your least-favorite
Christmas song on repeat
for two months
or
be banned from listening to all
Christmas music for a year?

WINNER: POINTS:

Would you rather
perform with the
Trans-Siberian Orchestra
or
the Rockettes?

WINNER: POINTS:

Would you rather
go to an amusement park
with the gang from
A Charlie Brown Christmas
or
The Muppet Christmas Carol?

WINNER: POINTS:

Would you rather
ride on Rudolph the Red-Nosed
Reindeer's back
or
build an igloo with
Frosty the Snowman?

WINNER: POINTS:

Would you rather
write the next hit Christmas song
or
a best-selling children's book
about the magic of Christmas?

WINNER: POINTS:

Would you rather
go on a beach vacation
with Heat Miser
or
a ski trip with the
Abominable Snow Monster?

WINNER: POINTS:

Would you rather
host a radio show where you count
down the best Christmas songs
or
a podcast where you discuss
classic Christmas movies?

WINNER: POINTS:

Would you rather
fall off the stage while singing
with the church choir
or
throw up in the middle
of the concert?

WINNER: POINTS:

Would you rather
hang out with Jack Frost
or
a group of Gremlins?

WINNER: POINTS:

Would you rather
do Christmas karaoke with
Alvin and the Chipmunks
or
Miss Piggy?

WINNER: POINTS:

Would you rather
rock around the Christmas tree at a
party with your school principal
or
your dentist?

WINNER: POINTS:

Would you rather
animate a Christmas cartoon
or
a Claymation movie?

WINNER: POINTS:

Would you rather
have Santa's laugh
or
the Grinch's sneer?

WINNER: POINTS:

Would you rather
live in a small town from a
Hallmark Christmas movie
or
at the North Pole?

WINNER: POINTS:

Would you rather
have the house to yourself like
Kevin McCallister in *Home Alone*
or
spend Christmas with the
zany Griswold family from
Christmas Vacation?

WINNER: POINTS:

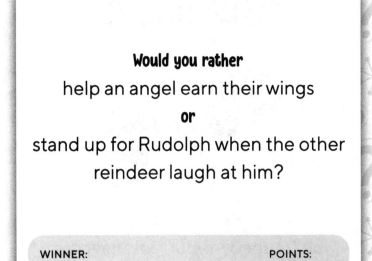

Would you rather

help an angel earn their wings

or

stand up for Rudolph when the other reindeer laugh at him?

WINNER: POINTS:

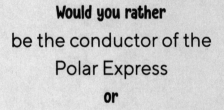

Would you rather

be the conductor of the Polar Express

or

the mayor of Whoville?

WINNER: POINTS:

Would you rather

be trapped in your least-favorite
Christmas movie

or

sing your least-favorite Christmas
song every day for a year?

WINNER: POINTS:

WINNER

ROUND 5

WINNER:

TOTAL POINTS:

ROUND

6

Santa's Workshop

Would you rather

find out that your dog is a reindeer

or

that your sibling is one of
Santa's elves?

WINNER: POINTS:

Would you rather

accidentally start a fire in
Santa's workshop

or

drop all the presents from
his sleigh on Christmas Eve?

WINNER: POINTS:

Would you rather

have one flying reindeer as a pet

or

20 pet reindeer that can
no longer fly?

WINNER: POINTS:

Would you rather

get a private tour of Santa's
workshop from Mrs. Claus

or

take a class from an elf on how to
build Christmas toys?

WINNER: POINTS:

Would you rather
bump into Santa
in your living room
or
watch his sleigh take off
from your roof?

WINNER: POINTS:

Would you rather
be the manager of Santa's workshop
or
the engineer for his sleigh?

WINNER: POINTS:

Would you rather

wake up one morning to find that
you've grown Santa's beard

or

reindeer antlers?

WINNER: POINTS:

Would you rather

be Santa's personal baker

or

hairstylist?

WINNER: POINTS:

Would you rather
manage Santa's
"naughty" and "nice" lists
or
map out his sleigh route
on Christmas Eve?

WINNER: POINTS:

Would you rather
permanently dress up like an elf
or
Santa?

WINNER: POINTS:

Would you rather

invent new toys for Santa's workshop

or

be the caretaker for his reindeer?

WINNER: POINTS:

Would you rather

step barefoot in reindeer poop

or

on a cluster of LEGO bricks?

WINNER: POINTS:

Would you rather
be Santa's assistant at all of his personal appearances

or

ride along in his sleigh when he delivers gifts?

WINNER: POINTS:

Would you rather
have a glowing red nose like Rudolph

or

angel wings?

WINNER: POINTS:

Would you rather
bake cookies with Mrs. Claus
or
play video games with an elf?

WINNER: POINTS:

Would you rather
have a toy from Santa's workshop
or
Santa's hat to show off to
your friends?

WINNER: POINTS:

Would you rather
go sledding at the North Pole
with a group of Santa's elves
or
ice fishing with a
talking polar bear?

WINNER: POINTS:

Would you rather
discover that Santa is mean
or
that you will receive coal in your
stocking this year?

WINNER: POINTS:

Would you rather
take Santa's sleigh for a
ride and crash it
or
get lost on it for two weeks?

WINNER: POINTS:

Would you rather
spend a week at Santa's workshop
but can't discuss it
or
see it for five minutes and be allowed
to tell your friends and family?

WINNER: POINTS:

Would you rather

read all the letters your friends
wrote to Santa

or

see if they made the
"naughty" or "nice" list?

WINNER: POINTS:

WINNER

ROUND

6

WINNER:
_____

TOTAL POINTS:
_____

ROUND

7

Winter Wonderland

Would you rather
have an ice rink in
your backyard
or
a ski slope?

WINNER: POINTS:

Would you rather
have snowflakes come out of
your eyes in place of tears
or
ice cubes?

WINNER: POINTS:

WOULD YOU RATHER?

Would you rather

walk through the snow wearing
fuzzy slippers

or

sandals?

WINNER: POINTS:

Would you rather

go snow tubing down Mt. Everest

or

dog sledding through the tundra?

WINNER: POINTS:

Would you rather

shovel a foot of snow using
an old sneaker

or

an ice cream scoop?

WINNER: POINTS:

Would you rather

run a race on a frozen pond
in sneakers

or

compete in a dance competition
wearing skates?

WINNER: POINTS:

Would you rather
have a giant snowball fight with your
neighborhood friends
or
with your class against
your teachers?

WINNER: POINTS:

Would you rather
eat a handful of dirty snow
or
an icicle that formed in
the local river?

WINNER: POINTS:

Would you rather
have a penguin for a pet
or
a snow leopard?

WINNER: POINTS:

Would you rather
build a snow fort
or
an ice sculpture?

WINNER: POINTS:

Would you rather
have your boogers turn
into icicles
or
your tongue stick to a
frozen flagpole?

WINNER: POINTS:

Would you rather
go snowboarding in your underwear
or
make a snow angel in your
bathing suit?

WINNER: POINTS:

Would you rather

jump into a freezing cold lake

or

hike five miles barefoot in the snow?

WINNER: POINTS:

Would you rather

be turned into a talking snowman

or

a singing polar bear?

WINNER: POINTS:

Would you rather
come face-to-face with a yeti
or
try to outrun an avalanche?

WINNER: POINTS:

Would you rather
get lost in the woods during
a blizzard
or
a hailstorm?

WINNER: POINTS:

Would you rather
race snowmobiles
or
Jet Skis?

WINNER: POINTS:

Would you rather
go snowboarding
blindfolded
or
skiing with your hands
tied behind your back?

WINNER: POINTS:

Would you rather
be able to create a blizzard
with your mind
or
melt ice and snow with
your hands?

WINNER: POINTS:

Would you rather
eat a snow cone filled with
dead bugs
or
bird feathers?

WINNER: POINTS:

Would you rather
live in a town where it flurries
every day
or
has a major blizzard five times
a year?

WINNER: POINTS:

WINNER: _____

TOTAL POINTS: _____

ROUND

8

Grab Bag

Would you rather
celebrate a white Christmas at home
or
a beach Christmas on a
tropical island?

WINNER: POINTS:

Would you rather
lose power in the middle of your
Christmas dinner at home
or
get snowed in at a relative's house
for three days?

WINNER: POINTS:

Would you rather

arm wrestle your strongest family
member for the last piece of pie

or

race them around the block?

WINNER: POINTS:

Would you rather

have a holiday bake-off
with your family

or

a Christmas scavenger hunt?

WINNER: POINTS:

Would you rather
have a food fight with your family
at Christmas dinner
or
a snowball fight after the meal?

WINNER: POINTS:

Would you rather
go caroling on Christmas Eve
or
have a snowman-building
competition on Christmas morning?

WINNER: POINTS:

Would you rather

participate in a board game
tournament on Christmas

or

compete in a series of
"Minute to Win It" games?

WINNER: POINTS:

Would you rather

spend Christmas with both sides of
your extended family

or

have a separate Christmas
celebration with each side of the
family?

WINNER: POINTS:

Would you rather
dress up like a character from a
Christmas movie
or
an animal that lives at
the North Pole?

WINNER: POINTS:

Would you rather
create an outfit constructed
solely from tissue paper
or
greeting cards?

WINNER: POINTS:

Would you rather
get sick on Christmas Eve and miss the family party
or
on Christmas morning and miss opening presents?

WINNER: POINTS:

Would you rather
attend a Christmas parade
or
concert?

WINNER: POINTS:

Would you rather
spend Christmas at
Disney World
or
in Hawaii?

WINNER: POINTS:

Would you rather
put on a funny Christmas pageant
with your family
or
reenact your favorite
Christmas movie?

WINNER: POINTS:

Would you rather

celebrate with a piñata full of Christmas-themed treats

or

toys?

WINNER: POINTS:

Would you rather

have a Christmas karaoke contest

or

play Christmas charades?

WINNER: POINTS:

Would you rather

spend Christmas in a cozy cabin on a snowy mountain

or

at a fancy hotel in a bustling city?

WINNER: POINTS:

Would you rather

knock over the punch bowl at your family Christmas party

or

the fondue pot?

WINNER: POINTS:

Would you rather
compete in a
gift-wrapping contest
or
Christmas trivia tournament?

WINNER: POINTS:

Would you rather
have a Christmas bonfire
or
cookie exchange?

WINNER: POINTS:

Would you rather

teach family members how to
make snow globes
or
build gingerbread houses?

WINNER: POINTS:

WINNER

ROUND

8

WINNER:

TOTAL POINTS:

This certificate
is awarded to

_____

for being marvelously merry,
fabulously festive, downright
dashing, and shockingly spirited!

Christmas magic has
nothing on you!

CONGRATULATIONS!

About the Author

 **Lindsey Daly** grew up in Andover, New Jersey. She graduated from Ramapo College of New Jersey with a BA in history and a certification in secondary education. Lindsey is a middle school social studies teacher and the author of *Would You Rather? Made You Think! Edition* and *Would You Rather? Family Challenge! Edition.* She lives with her dog, Teddy, in New Jersey.

Parents, for more information about Lindsey and her books, follow her online:

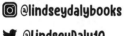

@lindseydalybooks

@LindseyDaly10

Hi, parents and caregivers,

We hope your child enjoyed *Would You Rather? Christmas Edition*. If you have any questions or concerns about this book, or have received a damaged copy, please contact customerservice@penguinrandomhouse.com. We're here and happy to help. Also, please consider writing a review on your favorite retailer's website to let others know what you and your child thought of the book!

Sincerely,
The Zeitgeist Team